ANCHOR BOOKS

THE CREAM OF EASTERN ENGLAND

Edited by

David Foskett

First published in Great Britain in 1996 by
ANCHOR BOOKS
1-2 Wainman Road, Woodston,
Peterborough, PE2 7BU

HB ISBN 1 85930 350 1
SB ISBN 1 85930 355 2

Foreword

Anchor Books is a small press, established in 1992, with the aim of promoting readable poetry to as wide an audience as possible.

The poems in *The Cream of Eastern England* represent a cross-section of style and content.

These poems are written by young and old alike, united in their passion for writing poetry.

I trust this selection will delight and please the authors from *Eastern England* and all those who enjoy reading poetry.

David Foskett
Editor

CONTENTS

SUNFLOWERS

A splash of orange on yellow background
With bits of green and bits of black
All the flowers coloured orange and gold
All mixed together in the palette of your soul.

One of many pictures in your house at Arles
Another piece to hang on the walls
The golden vase that bears your name
Stands on the canvas etched with pain.

Frenzied working, Gauguin coming
Desperate for companionship
Brighten up the visitor's room
Like my wall where hangs the print.

Then when I have the time to think
I see the madness
I feel the sadness
But it's beautiful . . . just beautiful.

Philip Telling

THE BEACH

On this beach I see the sea.
Wave upon wave against the shore.
On this beach the pebbles are many.
Always so quiet, always so clean.
People in summer, none in winter.
No house in sight, no car to hear.
On this beach the seagulls dwell.
Upon this beach I walk in peace.

Colin Gill

A SHOPPING SPREE ACCORDING TO ME

Mum said we'd go out shopping, I wondered what's in it for me,
I'm usually with my mummy, I'm not yet five you see.
I tower mum's knees thankfully, any shorter and I'd be crushed,
These shoppers all in a tearing hurry, 'Hang on now' what's the rush.
Pedestrians ever pushing past, and trampling on my toes,
And now I've got another problem, my cold and runny nose.
Mum's hanging onto my aching wrist, my clothes have come adrift,
My poor wee feet are aching bad, all this shopping has made me sad.

The supermarket is the worst, the trolleys all ways go,
Up the aisles into piles, of tins which were on show.
Smashing, grabbing ever dashing, like maniacs I saw,
Even the check-out kiosks are a laugh and annoy us all.
Mum wanted to pay by credit card, her limit struck a blow,
She reverted to a cheque book, the card out of date, oh no.
A phone call to Dad's office helped to save the day,
He's invited us out for lunch Yippee, Mum hopes he's going to pay.

Next the car park do we negotiate, every clown gets in Mum's way,
But patience is a virtue, so my Mum she used to say.
Like Mum's tumble dryer, my head spins round in gloom,
I often wonder what life's all about, and I expect you now do too.

Diana Dooner

CHRIST ALMIGHTY

A mean between two points
clasped at either end
in a vice
of our own making
or were we forsaken
by our imagined Christ?

Which part of our cross
were you nailed to?
You must have been at the top
and I at the bottom
Or were we inversed
or reversed
upside down
or torn inside out?

Our cross split
We bared our souls
Like Christ
with passion
Not objectively
but intensively
inwardly.

John M Pollard

TRUE LOVE

Two loving arms that hold you
Embracing you all night through
The comfort that's so precious
Loving sincere and true

Eyes that look deep into the heart
Encountering troubles that can tear you apart
The hurts from before are all in the past
You've found a love that you know will last.

Every day is a new beginning
Every day is a brand new hope
Every day a fresh understanding
Of new life with which you elope

L Loveland

AN UNBORN CHILD

A night of pleasure,
a night of fun,
results in thinking,
what have I done?

This unborn baby,
within me now,
brings about such feelings,
I don't know how!

But the feeling of love
abounds in me,
for this my child,
so small and wee!

I may not be married,
and yes I am young,
but my child will not suffer
for what people say is wrong.

Lesley Fuller

VAL

She had a special kind of grace
A happy smile, a lovely face
She was vain, and she was proud
She stood as one, the rest a crowd.

Time has rested gently upon her lovely face
But it has done nothing to mar her special grace
Maybe it's just illusion, perhaps not really there
But always in my mind's eye, she stays young and fair

N G Burt

THE GHOST VILLAGE

Where once a pretty village stood
Lie sharp black rocks, seaweed and wood,
The empty houses stand alone,
And late at night the wind does moan,
Then whistles through the walls;
The foaming waves hit the cliff -
Another section falls.
Now nothing is left but a few
Tin cans, oak planks and a church pew.
Still the storm waves batter on,
They won't stop 'til all is gone,
'Til all is lost beneath the sea,
When lifeless and lonely this coast will be.
There is no building left complete
Upon the shore where people meet,
Discussing their untimely fate
Whilst perching on a rotting crate.
The village rector sits alone,
Mumbling prayers in a mournful tone,
And staring fixedly out to sea,
He asks God why this had to be.
The sharp black rocks stand out starkly
Against the mist, it's whispered darkly
On cold nights when the wind is high,
That ghosts and spirits wander by,
Recalling memories of old times
And dancing to the church bell's chimes.
Scrambling over the jagged rocks,
A child whose youthful beauty mocks
The surrounding devastation
Falls down and cries with frustration,
And seagulls wheeling round the sky
Seem to shriek endlessly Why? Why?

Rifka McNair-Wilson

THE WORLD'S REAL D-DAY!

The light shone brighter than the sun itself,
Eyes melted under its intensity.
Old and young - their skin burnt away like paper,
Innocent civilians lost their lives.

From way up where the bomb was dropped
Death, damage and destruction could be witnessed.
The bomber was rocked by enormous blasts,
This was the start of the nuclear nightmare.

A huge nuclear cloud filled the sky,
A cloud from hell reached up to heaven.
Interested scientists watched on,
Japanese burned in their invention.

Thousands were wiped out, they lost their lives:
Old, young. Children, babies. Husbands, wives.
They died in a massive war fought by others,
They saved lives - their American brothers.

The war was won, Japan had been defeated,
But not the real enemy - *nuclear.*
Many Japanese had been out of order,
But did they all live in Hiroshima?
No!

Around the world the ultimate weapon's
Built - for security, though not of use,
Tons of the bastards - not one was fired,
Was there a point? They all felt threatened?

Now what? Nuclear bombs no longer needed?
All dumped in the sea - used on fishes,
Polluting as ever, killing again.
Achievement - a near nuclear 'cold' war.

The human race argues again, killing
The environment, using the power.
What's wrong? They never find a compromise;
Too intelligent, they'll kill us all!

Solution or revolution.

Hamish McNair-Wilson (15)

THE SEASIDE EXPRESS

The old railway station has long since gone;
No track or trains or bustling throng,
No porter or clerk, no booking hall,
Dust, smoke and noise are all swept away,
 - not even the cat's been permitted to stay!

Rows of neat houses now stand on the site,
 - no platform or buffet or waiting-room grim,
No luggage or mail, no clanging gates,
Just little gardens with hedges so trim,
Where horse and landau stood so patient and still.

But I've heard it said on a midsummer eve
A loud rumbling is heard disturbing the peace,
A crashing of brakes and explosion of steam
As the Seaside Express with a whistle so shrill
Thunders in and pulls up where the gates would have been.

Men, women and children in fashions so queer,
Disgorge from the carriages and rush to the pier,
Carrying buckets and spades and parcels of food,
That influx of visitors out on a spree,
Enjoying again their annual 'Wake' by the sea.

Rose E M Hilham

UNTITLED

Good-bye my dear friend,
You will never see the child that bears your name,
Nor touch again the land you hold so dear,
Now there is nothing left of you, but memories,
When we were boys at play, war was a game,
Dates in the pages of a book,
Forgotten history of a dim and distant past.

Good-bye my dear darling,
I hold your sweet face close to my breast.
You wait for my return, I fear it will not come,
But write to me of home, of England,
So that I may remember, the sweetness of bird song,
The quiet country lane, and flowers in the fields.

Good-bye brave soldiers, my comrades-in-arms,
Once we marched together,
Our hearts full of life and hope, and proud to serve,
What is there now but the stench of death,
Of gas and gunfire?
Where once young men stood,
Lie faceless empty shells.

Good-bye fair youth,
Your innocence has been taken,
Your generation all but gone,
There is no grave to mark your passing,
But one day, your name in stone will be carved,
A distant memory,
A hope for tomorrow,
A hope of peace.

Brenda Wilding

TEA BREAK

At ten o'clock the tea arrives.
I stand beside you at the desk.
The pulse, fast beating in your throat
It matches mine.

Your eye meets mine and winks.
The others there don't see.
The dark dilated pupil in your eye
It matches mine.

We talk and laugh, all three of us.
The air is charged with laughter.
Your hand is trembling as you smoke
It matches mine.

The tea is gone, the work begins.
Reluctantly I leave the desk.
The sadness you are feeling now
It matches mine.

Jenny Brennan

OBSERVATIONS IN A PUBLIC HOUSE

They now sit where we once used to be,
At a time when our zest for life
Was full of expectation and the innocence of youth.
As we listen to their natural laughter
And observe their smiles that radiate
The energy and excitement of the young,
We sit, glum faced, without conversation,
In a rut embittered by the years of life's experiences.
Recalling perhaps, in solitude, how there was a time,
When the roles were reversed.
And someone else was sitting here.
We then noticed their silent seriousness.
Do they see ours?
I wonder, will they have long distant dreams,
Destined never to be fulfilled,
With only the faded memories of earlier halcyon years
For company as old age approaches?

Michael Boast

HALF PAST SEVEN - NOVEMBER

Suddenly the sun
Made white gold by the mist
Burns through in mild surprise

Where fog had dogged my path
The vale had promised more
Yet morning met my eyes

Though not a proper valley
This Norfolk's flattened earth
Not someone else's world

Here fields will easy roll
Shallow terraced naked trees
Beyond the road unfurl

As greyness chased away
The milky sky pours on
And vastness, blue above, slips into view

Where plough has combed the soil
And pheasant runs to hide
For you dear son, this ancient world renew

Mike Saunders

DAY BREAK

Oft the chorus I have heard,
From the morning's early bird,
The richness of their tree-top song,
The joyous anthem of the throng.

A daily ritual of celebration,
Observing dawn's rejuvenation
From the blanketed night-time hour,
To daylight reaching budded flower.

The muted nightingale bestilled,
As daybreak's silent air is filled,
With choral song from after dark,
Sunrise is fire, but dawn the spark.

L'Argent

DREAM

Before dawn's early light,
Of yestermorn,
When dreamscapes form,
And nightmare chasms in imagination yawn,
Wrapped in burnished cloth of gold,
Stitched swiftly with silver thread,
Wizened dames to infants unfold,
Tales of fairy, witch and fantasy,
In my mind, eyes closed, but seeing,
Yarn of my making, maiden ecstasy,
But is it mine?
My mind in sleep a-roaming,
'Twixt the hours,
End in dawn, begin in gloaming,
Be gone my fears,
Haunting peace in daylight hours,
Banished with darkness,
Trouble me no more,
Night is for fairies,
Bath's good Wife's favoured lore.

Mark Lancaster

UNTITLED

No flowers by request, that's all it said,
Nothing to say when the service was
Just the announcement that he was dead, and
No flowers by request.

She dropped her head and softly said his name
Hoping that she could fight against her tears;
She wondered if he still held her to blame,
Though it was for the best.

What was his life, they hadn't kept in touch,
Since that day when she had made the choice,
Returning to her life that meant so much
'Better,' she said, 'this way.'

No flowers by request, she read again,
Tears fell from her eyes onto the page;
She hoped and prayed he hadn't suffered pain,
As he had done that day.

Ken Woodmason

6TH FEBRUARY, 1994

Dearest Lee,
Your spirit is free now,
Like a kestrel soaring in the sky,
Swooping, swerving, laughing and living,
Enjoying the feelings, touching and seeing,
Not trapped any more by walls of darkness,
Being able to walk, talk and hear.
Your love will always,
Be touching and refreshing,
To those who love you best.
At last now you can
See and feel what you couldn't before.
We will always love and be here for you,
Just call and we will listen.
Goodbye my love, goodbye.

Diana Steward

UNSPOKEN WORDS
Dedicated to all beloved dogs)

No need for spoken words,
A silent understanding is the link
Fulfilling that which needs-to-be,
'Twixt touching minds.

Though needs-to-be applied at times
An uttered word required - but brief,
Presenting then the cocked head
And quizzing brow.

Amber eyes so honest in portent,
Of that which never hints at lies.
Unity unquestioned in every way -
Could friendships draw on greater truth?

So short a span of treasured years slip by,
Draws blessed union to an end, so very swift.
The burning tears to precious loss,
Are caused to flow - but unashamedly.

In a world where fear and sadness rules,
Where human traits leave much to be desired,
So very hard to trust and give, in full accord,
Where love - so false at times, can be the all.

One single - so very honest glance can give
A sea of words unspoken.
A universe of love - united, so freely shown,
That which holds a special friend, so very close.

What wealth can buy such friends as those
Who at our side, doth linger long and true,
Through many years of sun and cloud,
Their depth of worth unplumbed?

Dennis F Tye

UNTITLED

She took a look behind her
Acknowledged her lost dreams
She left a life full of regrets
One fraying at the seams
The future would be brighter
Of that she seemed so sure
A life full of such misery
She couldn't face no more

Her suitcase held her treasures
Her heart held hopes and fears
Her mind was full of schemes and plans
But here eyes were filled with tears

She knew her destination
She knew what she would do
Her future held fulfilment
And a chance to start anew

A dingy bedsit somewhere
On the seedy side of town
A young girl's weeping sadly
For a life she never found
Now she sits and thinks back
To a life so far away
To those lost dreams she ran from
In a world called yesterday

Her suitcase held her treasures
Her heart held hopes and fears
Her mind was full of schemes and plans
But her eyes were filled with tears

She knew her destination
She knew what she would do
Her future held fulfilment
And a chance to start anew

Jennifer Moseley

TURMOIL

Object of my desire
You hold me still
Trapped in your spider web
You always will

Lover in my dreams
You love me still
But in the light of day
You never will

Betrayer of my trust
It pains me still
Knowing you walked away
And always will

Destroyer of my soul
I want you still
Try hard to break the spell
But never will

V A Elmer

PRELUDE TO AUTUMN

The shadows are lengthening
        Dawn comes not so soon
The time is approaching
        To see Harvest Moon
The sun's path sweeps lower
        When crossing the sky
Its light grows more golden
        As each day goes by
Days still can be balmy
        If weather is fair
Yet morning and evening
        There's chill to the air

Spring's leaves now look tired
        So dusty and worn
Soon from their branches
        By gales to be torn
But first to change colour
        A beautiful scene
Red, gold, brown and yellow
        Take place of the green
Fruits ripen and berries
        Of every kind
Are nature's own banquet
        That birds quickly find

The harvests are gathered
And fields ploughed once more
The hay and the straw stacked
For winter-time store
The swallows' nests empty
But no need to fear
A herald of spring-time
They'll be back next year
So cast away sadness
For summer that's flown
The autumn has loveliness
All of its own

Mandy Smith

MOTHER

You left without saying goodbye
Time snatched away from us
How cruel the reality of death
Stealing our closeness
Day by day
Aware of what you're missing
No cuddles
No touches
No sights or experiences.
They say time heals
But it never mends
The hole never fills
No matter how many friends
Conversation's one way
Don't dwell on what
Could have been
Facing the truth
Keep your pain
But accept what's happened.

Jean Barber

NO GOING BACK

It was set for high noon -
A sizzling day;
Sweat wet her forehead
And lay there like
Stultified tears.

He was fidgety, nervous,
His best suit frayed;
The 'bus had been late
And he prayed that she'd
Stay away.

Her pristine freshness
Had long gone stale;
She hoped he'd forgotten
As the dial of her watch
Showed him late.

But it wasn't to be
As they met at the door -
And each face mirrored grief
As it saw a past love
As a stranger.

Thelma Barlow

JASON

Oh! How I love that sweet happy sound
That greets me in the dawning,
The sound of my seven year old saying 'Good morning'.
He's slept so peacefully unaware of the strife
To get him what he wants for his little life,
He doesn't ask for much, a toy, a sweet,
A bit of love now and again
He doesn't know the strain,
He thinks money grows on trees or is made in banks.
I get a lump in my throat when I
Kiss him goodnight as he quietly whispers 'Thanks.'

Joslin Griffiths

MY BROTHER

I visit once a week,
Up the concrete steps, through the dismal hall,
Up the narrow dusty stairs.
His room is fairly decent, a bed, wash-basin, chair.
How will he be today? I hardly dare to knock,
I shrink from his despair.
Sometimes he'll chat, though always full of woe,
Sometimes he's so in pain, he flings his body on the
bed, he doesn't say hello.
At seventeen his mind was good, exceptionally bright.
Some quirk of nature picked him out, some schizophrenic blight.
Mum used to cry, and ask me why it had to be her son.
Was it something *she* had caused, something *she* had done.
I climb the stair, I know his chance of being cured is zero,
But he's still there, he smiles today, he is my unsung hero.

Joan Ross

INTIMATE

In movement . . .
through chaotic whisper . . .
obscene . . . my love . . .
obscene . . .
amidst devotions . . .
good . . . new . . . darkness . . .
how soft this sickness burns
these seams . . .
come winter . . . my seclusion . . .
come victim . . . after victim . . .
come . . .
to become the blood's
intrusion . . .
the skin's despair . . .
the breath's rhythm . . .
come . . . wither . . . within . . .
my damp embrace . . .
come . . . gather me into . . .
your sweet decay . . .
come . . . drain my eyes . . .
of all their blue . . .
for I have come . . .
to drain . . .
from you . . .

Russell Patient

THE MIRACLE OF BIRTH

I can remember the day she was born.
In the early hours of a Tuesday morn.
The long nine month wait had seemed hard to bear
I couldn't believe she was really here.
The pain so unbearable at its height
Forgotten at last, as with great delight,
I counted her fingers and all her toes.
She looked very perfect, with upturned nose.
So small and so wrinkled with screwed up eyes
It was hard to believe, this heav'n sent prize.
Her dear little hands with fists clenched up tight.
Opening eyes, getting used to the light.
I cradled her snugly against my breast
Gave an extra hug for this new-born guest
Who had now arrived, bringing untold joy
(It had mattered not whether girl or boy.)
'Twas then that I knew through all pain and strife
Creation's wonder, had brought me new life.
Last night, this child had depended on me.
Her life now her own, in our family.
With tears of joy I then thanked God above,
For sending this babe, to cherish and love.

Gwynneth Howard

SEPTEMBER

The mellow days, the soft warm air,
The lawn is drenched with dew.
The early morning mists arise,
September days we cannot disguise.

Early evening shadows fall,
The days speed swiftly by.
We sense approaching changes,
At dusk a pale pink sky.

A rose will linger here and there,
Chrysanthemums will bloom.
Sweet peas of deep and pastel shades,
Still decorate our home.

The summer days have cast their spell,
Intangible it seems,
September clinging wistfully,
Will halt the summer dreams.

Through the months of summer,
September holds the key,
To nature's coming changes,
To us life's mystery.

Dorothy Wales

THE CANDLE LIGHT KEEPS BURNING

The candle light is just burning there.
Waiting for your smiling face to arrive here.
Will you come? I do not know.
But I'll just sit here and hope you show.

It seems a long while since I've been waiting.
Shall I give up and blow out the candle, that's what I'm debating.
But my heart says no, give it a while longer.
I give in and have a drink, something stronger.

What is this I see? You've arrived at last.
Oh no! I awake and know I've been dreaming of the past.
I realise that together for now we will never be.
But I know the candle still burns while you wait for me.

Kathy Buckley

LA PLAGE - THE BEACH

The lighthouse beams across the landscape,
Scavenging seagulls scouring the sandy beaches.
The salty, lingering air,
The taste of cockles and mussels on my tongue.
The wind blowing through my hair.
Noisy ships passing to and fro.
Children excitedly playing in the sea,
The beach is such a happy place.

People burying their pinkish feet,
Mum's trying to get a tan,
The usual old people on the seats,
A teenager drinking a can.

Summer's over now,
Autumn's nearly here.
Happy times are shared by everyone,
Gazing off the pier.

Sarah Clarke (14)

PROTECTORS OF THE INNOCENT

May those who are intent on war
Not rule the nations any more;
But those who foster lasting peace
And justice, in their power increase.

May those who still intend to fight
Have no authority or might;
Those who protect the innocent
Rule over every continent

May those intent on greed and hate
Be seen not as the good and great;
But as our rulers those succeed
Who help the poor and those in need.

May those ambitious for self gain
Not rule o'er any race again.

Lily Jakubowski

DON'T CRY

Do not cry nor sob and shed a tear for me,
I have not gone, I still remain, I'm all around you see?
In the rustling of the leaves you'll sometimes hear me sigh,
When shadows fall, could it be, it's me that passes by?

At the rising of the sun you'll think of me and smile,
In dreams I'll come to stay with you, but only for a while.
We'll talk the old times over, of then and when and now,
We'll both discuss the reasons and why and who and how.

These years we've been together and now it's time to rest,
A journey full of love and joy and, you, you were the best.
With such a happy family, was I really very shy?
Please tell them all I'm peaceful now, and say a fond goodbye.

A final word to you my dear, a last word and it's this,
I'm glad I lived my life with you, a story not to miss.
My love lives bright and shiny, a warm and mystic light,
Don't fear sleep or the darkness, keep loving me each night.

Don't cry for me, remember, I have not gone you see!
Be happy with your memories, of them and us and me.
I know I'm in your heart and mind, a roaming in your dreams,
I have not gone, I'm all around and still with you it seems.

Live your life, be happy, don't cry a tear nor weep,
To watch out for you always, is a promise that I'll keep.
Our love transcends all boundaries across the great divide,
What was, like now, and yet to be, I'll be there by your side.

Joseph Gregory

TOLLESBURY ON REMEMBRANCE DAY

Are you watching, British Tommies,
from somewhere up above?
Do you see the tiny village square
in the country that you love?
Do you see the little children
hand in hand and two by two
lay their posies on the ground
in memory of you?
If you do then you'll be smiling
as they laugh and skip and play
for reverence and innocence
are strangers anyway.

Are you watching, British Tommies,
silent and unseen?
Do you see the growing families,
the pub, the village green?
The quiet and lonely marshes
reach out and touch the sea
still unchanged and beautiful,
still British and still free.

Though we talk in terms of valour,
of conquerors and kings,
I believe the British Tommy died
to save the simple things.
And as we all pay tribute
in silent requiem
the flowers of the children
will mean the most to them.

Tom May

A MOTHER'S PEACE

I lay upon the shingled beach,
With a towel thrown on the ground.
My lumps and bumps protruding
As I listened to every sound.

The children splashing in the sea
Shouting 'Mum oh Mum, look at me.'
They yelled and screamed with such delight
Jumping the waves with all their might.

What happened to the peace and quiet
Of being on one's own?
You couldn't, wouldn't like it
And yes you'd only moan.

For our children are very special
Even when they are a pain
For we would not be without them
And their noise is our blessed gain.

Lesley Byfield

RAIN

Each droplet starting high in the cold sky against
A dark silhouette of rippling movement.
100,000 droplets dancing like tiny ballerinas
Whose flowing movement is orchestrated by the
Wind to a crescendo at the storm's eye.

Wave after wave dancing across the ground driven
By an unseen hand, growing to fever-pitch then
At its height, it abates.
Slowing, quieting, calming to a slight patter
Against the glass, until it escalates into a
Second symphony of howling noise as the storm rages
A path across the ravaged land.

Each perfect sphere falling to earth with
Unrelenting determination whereupon it explodes
Into another thousand spheres joining together
To form a living, flowing river.

Whose power can give or take away the very
Nature of life as it flows across the hard dry earth?
On its way home to its parent the sea before
Once again it is snatched away by the merciless
Blowing wind.

Geoff Baker

LOVE

Love,
There are different kinds.
The love between boys and girls
but sometimes this is blind.

The love in your family
will always be there
and the love for your neighbour or a stranger
is shown with care.

There's love between husband and wife.
There is love all through your life.
there is love between young and old
but sometimes love can be cold.

How do we know if love is real?
By the way we touch or the way we feel?
There is no explanation of what love is
But love is often shown with a hug or a kiss.

But sometimes love goes astray
leaving behind the hurt and betrayed.
But the love that will always be
is the love between you and me.

Kate Ann Milne (14)

AUTUMN

There is a slight chill in the air, the days are not so long.
It says soon winter will be here and summer nights are gone.
The trees are dressed in golds and browns, their leaves before they fall,
are dancing in their autumn gowns, their end of season ball.

The sun she rises late these days to dry the glistening dew,
but misty clouds keep out her rays, for bright clear days are few.
And soon Jack Frost will come again to breathe a frosty sigh,
and cloudless skies give way to rain as autumn says goodbye.

Ruth Bowles

FREEDOM

Don't you understand
Freedom is yours!
It is wide open.
The plains run far.
The only snares are
Your mind.
Then why is this house
Not of glass but
Thick black mud?
To liberate this flesh
I have done.
But these thoughts
Double back to the mud.
In the morning I will say;
'Run mind run'
And in my bed the mud puts
Me to rest.

Chris Cutter

FOSSIL STONE

Metal and gold with holes?
Black bugs - dark circle -
Like a trilobite -
Memories of old -
Memories of school - of biology
Embedded in our minds.
This fossil stone -
This ageless rock -
Of heights and steps -
Forever entwined
Dark, but smiling
This shiny blackness -
This 'snail' this mite -
Of sharpness.
For this is not a square
So hidden within - personal.
Ancestors -
With no beginning no end -
Just existing.

E J Faraday

DEEPER THAN COLOUR

Love should run deeper than colour
When cut we all bleed red
Why can't we help one another
And join together as friends?

In a world that's so fruitful
It's surely a sin
We share the same planet
But that's where it ends

I'm hoping for sunshine
As you're praying for rain
While I'm seeking pleasure
All you have is pain

I watch the sun rise with promise
You watch it go down in vain
We all have our problems
But I just can't complain

Colin Lee Boyd

CARDBOARD CITY

He has no home, no place to stay,
He has no parents to guide him the way,
When he was ten his parents died,
He didn't want to live with anyone else so he lied.

He lied about his name being Scott Carter,
He lied that he had a mother and father,
So now he lives in a cardboard city,
All day and night, where the streets are dirty.

He sleeps in a box, somewhere in the gutter,
He lies there at night among all the clutter,
During the day he roams the streets,
Searching the city for a bite to eat.

His clothes are dirty, his clothes are ripped,
He has no buttons, he has no zips,
No zip on his jacket, no patches on his knees,
He has holes in his clothes as everyone can see.

There's no one out there, no one who cares,
Everyone walks past, and everyone stares.

C A Mott

EMOTIONS

Love and hate go hand in hand,
Things never turn out the way you planned;
We feel good, we steal a kiss,
Never dreaming all this could amiss.

Emotions are high, the world will know,
How much we love each other so;
Oh! Such dreams, such happiness,
Nights to share, children to bless.

Round the corner hate hides away,
Waiting patiently till the right day;
Just one wrong move, a misused word,
Hate slowly creeps up, silent, unheard.

Love should be spoken, love should be seen,
Day after day work as a team;
One bad moment, one little tiff,
Could easily end in a marital rift.

Slowly we grow further apart,
Neither of us having the heart;
To say what we feel, to let them know,
The things they do, just hurt you so.

Time then comes when we speak no more,
Daily happenings become a bore;
We look around for something to do,
Our thoughts start straying for someone new.

This is where hate puts itself fore,
Never far, just behind the door;
He pushes you right over the edge,
What was it you vowed in your marriage pledge.

It's so easy to say, easy to do,
But don't let all this happen to you;
Stay young lovers all your life,
Push hate away and end the strife.

G Horne

MATTER OF FACT

Saw a man just the other day
Looked into the air and blew his cares away
Twenty five years in a string of jails
Pain for security in case all else fails

Sweet little face and so out of place
Been let down hurt
By the whole human race
Saw that child as a matter of fact
Ready to make the devil's pact
Matter of fact
It was just yesterday
Led my heart
Into dismay

Woke up from sleep the other night
Broke the heart of the torch of the burning light
Matter of fact been so blind
Matter of fact lost the only thing I could find

Sweet little face in a nine to five
Working so hard
Just so she can stay alive
Saw that girl as a matter of fact
Fulfilled her part of the devil's pact
Matter of fact
It was just yesterday
Took my heart
And then gave it away

Matter of fact
The sun don't shine
Matter of fact
It's all out of time
Matter of fact
Don't know what to do
Matter of fact
I love you.

Daryl Tomlinson

MOMENTS ONLY FOR THE PRESENT

Now is the time -
that you are in my thoughts
as I board the train.
Maybe it will be alright
again.
Maybe, who knows?

Now is the hour -
before I reach my destination
that is your home town.
Maybe it will be alright
next time around.
Maybe, who knows?

Now is the minute -
away from going down the steps -
leading to the High Street.
Maybe it will be alright
when we meet.
Maybe, who knows?

Now is the split second -
approaching your house
to ring your door bell.
Maybe it will be alright
when we meet.
Maybe, who can tell?

Marianne Welsh

FRIEND

You do not ask for mighty deeds or sacrifice,
Nor wondrous temples rising to the sky,
You do not ask of us to pay the highest price,
You'd never ask a trembling mouse to fly!

You know our fears and meet our deepest needs with love
Knowing our weakness and our puny frame,
Sending your Holy Spirit like a gentle dove
To help us use your mighty power and holy name.

When in fear we come to you, trembling with our shame
For all the things wherein we failed to shine
You call us gently, quietly yet forcefully by name
And say, 'But don't you know the glory is all mine?'

You're always there to lift the tired despairing heart
You never scold in anger, or rebuff
A child of yours who tries to take his lowly part
Yet fails, because the path he chose is rough.

You rescue us from all our self-inflicted fears,
Your presence like a soothing balm,
You hold us carefully through all our stumbling years
And keep us in the hollow of your palm.

M Lander

COULD THIS BE ME?

Alone again,
Has time forgot,
This special person,
Who's found himself without the lot?

He had his home,
His family too,
Life looked so bright,
So much for him to do

Alas, now all he's lost,
For him at such a cost,
But who are we to complain,
When we meet this person again,
After all, me, you, we may soon
Be the same.

I Bromidge

LOVE

Davey my beloved
Stormed the raging sea
Rocked my heart with that smile
Hair with waves, wild and free.

He was a poet in the making
Played a guitar for me in style
Singing for him I was nervous and quaking
For those blue eyes I fell for in a while.

Such passion how I love him to be near to me
Embracing arms, instant liking,
Makes me closer to thee.

From the very start he touched my heart
I felt like a school girl whisked off my feet
And fancy free
Oh thanks Davey for what you've offered,
And your hospitality,
Such wonderful days spent with me.

M Jowsey

THE MIRROR

Look who is in there staring back at me,
Open my eyes wide in order to see,
The shock that I feel when I notice the pain,
The mirror showing me the time that I gain.

Look in the mirror and what can I see?
An abandoned lost soul staring right at me,
The years of old torment are etched in deep lines,
The reality and the truth of the quickness of time.

Look in the mirror and who's face is seen there?
The screwed-up expressions are years of my cares,
Watching me slowly intent upon my face,
Take a look inside at the lonely black space.

Look in the mirror and what can I tell?
This person is fighting the cobwebs of spell,
Look in the mirror and what can I see?
At last a found soul that rests peacefully.

Samantha Murdoch

FEAR

Darkness drops
Like a black velvet curtain
Before my eyes.
Panic prevails;
Shamefully seeping
through my skin,
Hanging,
Heavy,
Hovering.
The smell of fear.
A rough hand coils
around my neck;
Scales sending shivers
Down my spine.
To my feet.
Wrists forced together;
Cold silver links
like a serrated blade
Cut into my flesh.
And I bleed.
Black sticky blood
dripping down,
Down my legs;
A snail trail
Glistening through the dark.

Jane H Skoulding

SAND BARGES BRIGHTLING SEA

Early morning, two or three
Peering past the point to see
A green light standing in.

Now we hear her steady beat
Merging with the far off bleat
Of restless sheep, across the fields.

Up darkened creek, she feels her way
Past misty saltings, edged with clay
Losing the battle with rising tide.

Close to the jetty now she glides
The mate's dark shadow, at her sides
Stand by me lads, for ropes.

Rumble of engine, taking off her way
Bump of steel on fender, creak of rope, and stay
Silent now the motor, silent as the night.

Now run the motors from ashore
Driving belts that run for evermore.
At last, at last! Cheers lads, the loading's done.

G Neale

TO THE FERRY

To the ferry, walking
Quickly, wind stalking
Close, buffeting the sea
And cloud-raking,
Red sails breaking
Up the blue

One boat halted,
Lying tilted,
On the monster-hump
Man thigh-high in the sump
Sunday wading,
Fun-day fading

Dodging dog-walkers
And earnest talkers
Conversation snatches
Caught in patches
And thrown
By the playful wind

Martello tower high
Breaking up the sky,
Somersaulting kites
Appear, invite
Our eyes to chase
Their crazy race

Slowing to watch,
Lingering on the beach,
Forgetting the hurry
Of getting
To the ferry

M Garvey

FATHER

You're part of my reality
I cannot touch you
Losing my sanity
Or can I feel you
I'm no reflection in your eyes
My truth within you lies
Do you see me?

Your voice a thought inside my head
Keeps me from sleep
Memories like a guilty child
Do quietly creep
Footsteps softly fall
In the mind's eternal hall
Do you hear them?

I stride into the winter air
And chase my breath
Watch it quickly disappear
As if in death
Like yourself it may seem gone
But it truly lingers on
I can feel it.

P J Frowen

PLAYING WITH FIRE

A hot, wet tear tumbles
Down the slope of her cheek,
Leaving a salty grey stream,
Of mascara marking its journey.

Thoughts and feelings chase each other
Around her head in a confused temper,
As a lump slowly forms in her throat,
And her heart snaps and cracks in two.

After one sunshine filled afternoon,
Love had dashed swiftly into her life,
But had apparently been absent from his,
Still filled with dark clouds of doubt.

As the phone refuses to ring
With his promised call,
Despair and self doubt settle in for the night,
To add thunder to the storm of emotions.

The smouldering spark of desire is stamped out,
As hope is fought to the floor.
Her feelings are guarded by a cool exterior,
Reserved for times of rejection.

Now battered and bruised, she will go back for more,
Once the healing touch of morning has set in.
But how long does it take to accept
A one sided love affair for what it is?

No more than a dangerous game.

Clare Smith

A FISHY TALE

We have Terry come to visit.
With blue car and trailer,
He brings us fish all fresh and clean.
We say well hello sailor.
He chats with girl Fennella,
I hope that this will do.
A lovely piece of fish to grill,
Is that okay for you?
Another day he sees girl Dot,
Now she really is a tease,
Boy Terry says smoked fish me dear,
Our Dot she's really pleased.
We have a laugh together,
As boy Terry he will say
Now Janet when I bring the prawns,
Will you be dressed on Saturday?
He goes along to do his rounds,
With hat and coat of white
And people they are really pleased,
He is a welcome sight.
He calls at Don and Edna's.
Cause they like fish it's true.
Prawns, shrimps and crabsticks,
Cause they're really good for you.
He sells so many sorts of fish,
It's difficult to choose.
So now you know our Terry,
You we wouldn't want to lose.

Janet Tovell

A DAY AT FELIXSTOWE

The sea is shimmering in the sun,
Lazily, it laps along the shore
Like the sound of music, as it turns
The little waves - and its course is run.
She carries the yachts gently over the tide,
The sailboards go steadily gliding along,
Truly the sea is a wonderful place,
And that's what I love to be in.
To plunge in the water and feel so refreshed
Whilst swimming below, and above,
To lie on my back looking up at the sky,
Watch the little white clouds sailing merrily by.
There are many big ships passing by each day
Tor Britannia, Beatrix, Oberon too
Dana Anglia, Winston Churchill, sailing away
New container ships come into view.
And here on the beach, children having such fun
As the spades and the buckets come out,
Making castles and puddings from out of the sand
Then the sea washes them down one by one.
The people all lie in bikinis and shorts,
They are trying to turn their skins brown,
Then the seagulls go searching for food on the beach
That the folk have left lying around.
And now comes the time to pack up and go
Back to the noise of the town,
Leave the peace of the sea, and the warmth of the sun
But be sure we will be back again!

Cindy Gibbons

MEMORIES

The old man sat, shoulders bent, energy spent,
Listening to the waves, lapping the shore,
Each one so new, so sure,
He thought of his youth, when he was strong,
Of his first love, now sadly gone.
Of the time they ran barefoot in the sand,
Walking in the rain, hand in hand,
Hair blowing in the breeze,
Wind whistling in the trees.
A smile crosses his face.
So many memories in this place,
Day dreams done, time to move on.
He pats the dog, waiting by his side,
His companion, friend, also his guide.
'Take me home boy, home to tea,
Where we can curl up by the fire together, you and me.'

Myrtle Elden

TRAPPED

I lie awake with tears in my eyes
Trying not to think of you. Only trying
I can't get you out of my head
I lie here wishing that I was dead
Your absence is venomous

I am trapped in a tower
With a solitary view.
I know that if you stay with me tonight
Tomorrow everything will be alright.
Why do I feel like this?

I now longer know what is real.
Hell I don't even know how I feel.
No matter how bad things are now
We will work it out somehow.
But right now, I am sick of trying.

I am trapped in a tower
With a solitary view.
Nothing for company, but a plain white dove
Spreading out its wings of love
Why do I feel like this?

I never wanted to let you back inside
But I lost count of all the tears I've cried
I don't need this pain any more
Everything you said was false
Get out of my head

I am trapped in a tower
With a solitary view
I know that if you stay with me tonight
Tomorrow everything will be alright
Please stay with me
Make everything alright.
Why do I feel like this?

G Miers

THE MORNING AFTER

The morning after the night before
Beer cans strewn across the floor
Empty glasses by the score
I lay in bed, my head is sore
The price of whisky, wine galore
The price of turning in at four
The girl I danced with, what a whore
The girl I danced with starts to snore
I don't know what I do it for
The ugliest girl you ever saw
Asleep beside me, in the raw
Saliva dribbling down her jaw
We danced, we kissed of that I'm sure
I can't remember any more
It's time to run, make for the door
Oh how I really do abhor
The morning after the night before.

Jon Dyer

DREAM TIME

As I lay asleep in bed,
Strange stories fill my sleeping head.
I dream of Sundays crammed with fun,
Of bright days filled with games and sun,
I dream of sea shores, castles high,
Of sparkling seagulls flying by,
Of unicorns upon the sand,
With me upon their backs so grand,
White fluffy foam on waves so high,
That turn to clouds high in the sky.
All happy dreams throughout the night
Ensure I sleep secure and tight.

J Byrne

MY DAD

My dad is a great chess king,
A tall giraffe, a bit of a laugh,
A lovely silver wedding ring,
He's a funfair man,
Happy and kind,
And I'm glad,
'Cause he's all mine.
My dad is friendly and jumpy,
A rocking horse, a humpty dumpty,
He's optimistic, ample and brave,
When he's asleep he's as dead as a grave,
But sometimes he's a *go to bed now*,
A *hurry up* and *shut the door*,
A cross old bat, a bit of a bore,
He tells me off but says no more,
And I'm just glad, 'cause he's a great dad.

Karen Maton (11)

TIL EULENSPIEGEL

The pulse of this earth's sorrow
Beats through our happiest cadences.

Sweet flowing sequences
Break into clashing discords of dismay.

The shadow's edge
Invades our dearest silences,

And empty caverns yawn
Beneath the strongest footholds.

The carefree run of youth
Spills into jangled chaos of lost illusions.

The cynic's smile twists
Through the tragic comedy of errors;

And laughter, glad uproarious laughter
Is caught and gallowed on the mocking tree.

M Cornish

HOPE

The wheels of life are turning,
Even as we recall . . .
The painful sting of yesterdays,
The sadness of it all.

The wheels of life keep turning
Bringing new hope every day,
The memories fade to shadows
But the scars won't go away.

The wheels of life still turning,
New loves, new friends, new goals,
Happiness rules over grief,
Healing injured souls.

The wheels of life continue
Beyond the time of man,
So take your life into your hands
And enjoy it - whilst you can.

Tina Cheshire

AUTUMN TIME

Apples are ripe now on the trees
Brown leaves are rustling in the breeze
Yes Autumn's here in all its glory
Every year the same sweet story
The countryside has turned to gold
A pretty sight now to behold
A special season yes that's clear
It is a lovely time of year
The fields will soon be hung again
With soft grey mists that turn to rain
Then suddenly as if by cue
The Autumn sunshine will break through
On grass and hedges down the lane
Dewdrops hang from last night's rain
And spiders' webs oh what a sight
Like lacy patterns fine and light
Yes Autumn's here and Summer's gone
So soon our thoughts will turn upon
Winter time with fires ablaze
So make the most of Autumn days

Janet Knights

THE LONELY SHORE

The holiday's over and they're back to school.
No boys to fish in the rocky pool,
No girls to *busy* with all this sand,
No cousins or brothers or dads at hand.
No mums to sort the family out,
No tiny tots to splash about.
It's sad they've had to leave the sea
To the sun and the wind and the waves - and me.

The night tide's captured and swept away
The castle and pies of yesterday,
And washed the sand all smooth and flat.
No sign of kite or cricket bat.
And cooling waves with lacy foam
Lick at my feet as I walk alone,
And turn and twist as they reach the shore,
All racing to catch the one before.

Then, like a queen I sit alone,
A million pebbles are my throne,
Myriads of diamonds sparkle my sea,
And the gold of the sun caressing me.
My music the lilt of the rhythmic tides,
And the cry of the gull as it searching, glides.
My kingdom stretches as far as the eye,
As great ships along the horizon ply.

Christine Day

TINY

You are a creation,
You have such tiny feet,
Tiny hands, and a tiny nose,
Tiny bright eyes open for the first time,
Tiny ears hearing sounds of all kinds.

You are so tiny so very precious too,
You are a unique creation,
Growing up to become you,
Everyone will watch you grow,
Through the different stages,
Your caring family
Fussing around your ages.

But now, you are so precious, days a blur,
Soon you will know where you are,
In great loving care,
Little one don't worry,
For love will fill your world,
Your mum and dad will protect you,
So strong you soon will be.

Although you will never remember,
You were born so tiny, so perfect too,
Made all our happy hearts cry,
For you took a wonderful
Place in time.

All the joy and love and luck, of life,
We wish your way,
Know for these first confusing days,
Just open up your eyes,
Look your mother's way,
For held there, within her eyes,
Is the light and love of life,
For now, that's all you need to know,
And that will help,
You,
A tiny unique creation,
To grow.

Suzanne Tattersall

THE HIGH STREET RACETRACK

Life's just a blur,
As people hurry scurry flurry
Their way along;
Each intent on their own
Secret purpose.

Frantic dashing, never crashing,
In and out they weave.
Heads down
Minds fixed;
Each intent on their own
Secret purpose.

I sit and watch
The seconds and the season
Ticking ticking *ticking*
Hastily away.
The pendulum swings busily
Marking metronomic minutes.

Torrents of humanity
Wash way over me.
People going flowing never slowing.
Rapid pace, must win the race
No-one ever stopping
'Cause they are, all so intent
On their Christmas shopping.

Jane Nower

THE MIRROR GAME

I looked in the mirror,
What did I see
A little girl
Dressed in red,
Just like me.
Her hair was golden,
Her eyes were blue.
I ran to tell Mummy,
She said, 'That is you.'

Once more in the mirror
I could see
Myself standing upright,
Straight as could be.
I moved an arm,
I raised a leg,
And in the mirror
I could see,
That mirror was playing a game with me.

So what did I do?
I made a face,
Touched my nose,
Scratched my head,
Pulled an ear,
And laughed out loud,
Mummy came running,
And laughed to see
The mirror was playing a game with me.

Jessie Burgess

SPRING 86

Dearest Libby, don't be down
Don't live your life behind a frown,
Get right up, give it a whack,
That's how to do it, go on *attack*!

Dearest Libby, don't despair
You must know that we all care.
Things will change, they will improve
All you need is faith and love.

Faith to do what you think best;
Go and put them to the test!
Love yourself and the world will follow
Nothing's ever quite that hollow.

Chris Medhurst

MY WONDERLAND

When I wander through the meadows
In the early morning light,
I see the silver threads of the spiders' webs
Bejewelled by the tears of night,
I hear the distant rising fish,
The stirring birds awake
As the silent tree waits patiently
For the breeze, his sounds to make.

The owl now his hunting done,
Returns not quite alone
But the prey he holds for his hungry young
Will not be going home.
The meadow lark is first to rise,
And soars to sing on high,
I'm sure he sings of the beauty seen
From his platform in the sky.

Near the steaming placid stream
A flash of metal blue,
A gentle splash, the minnow held,
Breakfast time for two.
Kingcups and forget-me-nots hide between the reeds,
In the marshy fringes by the stream
Where countless insects breed.
Soon the graceful dragonfly will start his busy day
Visiting each reed or flower he chooses on his way.

I will never cease to wonder at this beauty I behold,
As I watch this waking wonderland, unfold.

R G Rudd

NOTHING LASTS FOREVER

Nothing last forever,
All things pass away.
How do you catch a sunbeam
Or make a rainbow stay.
How do you catch the soft soft breeze
That rustles through your hair,
One minute you have a snowflake,
And the next it isn't there.
How can you hold
The sun's red glow
As it sinks behind a mountain;
How can you capture the water
That gleams and glistens in a fountain.
How can you keep the fragile child
From growing to a man.
How can you cease the tireless sway
Of waves upon the sand.
Oh! But no-one can catch a sunbeam
Or make a rainbow stay,
Nothing lasts forever, all things pass away.

Lucy Peacock

THE WAY IT WAS

If I were to speak with you
Of the distant rounded hilltops,
Of the crisp-white virgin snow,
Of the journey further north,
Of the glorious autumn day.

If I were to speak with you
Of the watery deep-red sun,
Of the casting cloak of hue,
Of the rising hints of dusk,
Of the secret hideaway.

If I were to speak with you
Of the love I share beside me,
Of the gentle hand in mine,
Of the welling from within,
Of the words we need not say.

If I were to speak with you
Of the focus of our minds,
Of the oblivion that surrounds,
Of the times our dreams come true,
Of the solitude we pray.

If I were to speak with you
Of all these things . . .
Never could the brush be moved
Nor the canvas coloured
Nor the picture painted
Of the love we share between us
Of the scene I would portray.

David Redwin

MY HOMECOMING

Will the garden gate still squeak to me
That friendly old Hello!
And the sun shine on the concrete path
Near where the tulips grow.

Will there be song in the knocker's bang
When I get back from *Rome*
Will Mum's tears and Dad's firm grip
Say 'Son you're welcome home.'

And the silent words in Uncle's eyes
As we come face to face
Still glow with joy that we both knew
Even time could not erase.

They will all be the same to me
These folks that I adore
And then I'll say 'God Bless You Mum,
But you're all worth fighting for.'

It's a long time since I left them
And only Uncle knew
That I was bound for overseas
Across the dangerous blue.

Good luck has been with me always
In these foreign lands
Whilst living in Italian mud
Or in the African sands.

Albert C Gray

PIN CUSHIONED

Innocents, devotion, pure being,
Crushed by the liquid of society,
Designer minds, throbbing tones
Forced into lines of modern ecstasy.
Deluded people of love
Moulded souls of emptiness.
Tempted creatures of contrived lives
Controlled without knowledge.
Believing in freedom
Entombed behind walls
Built by governors of tyranny.
Caught without realisation
Like animals born in captivity.

Fiona Leggo

THE LANC

Lincolnshire's the place to be
Down at RAF Coningsby

People come from miles around
Just to hear the glorious sound

The Lanc stands there so large and tall
No mistaking the engines' roar.

She flies with grace across the sky
Knowing she helped us get by

So come on down to Coningsby
You never know you just might see
This lovely plane with wings so wide
Standing there in all her pride.

V Evans

PEN DINAS

Do you - or are you blind - not see
This land shining in the evening air?
Calm, steady, peaceful, though but transitory,
From this I draw a short serenity,
And call those fools who manufacture fears,
And frighten others, needlessly,
And much is needless, much need never be.

M Daniels

ON BEING A SOCIAL WORKER

What's the problem?
I haven't got a problem
Everybody's got a problem
Well, I haven't got a problem.
Well maybe that's your problem.

Martin Smith

FEBRUARY FUNERAL

He was there -
In the flesh he'd
Grown out of,
Wasted;

Not standing on ceremony,
But lying rapt
In cerements.

Lying severed from his living,
In the puppet-box;

Waxen, wooden -
Lidded.

Eyes and pine
Pinned with pining,

Everything grave
In the ground

And gravity arising.

* * *

I am here -
On the lighter side
Of his weighted door,
But he is not

And nothing more:

Nothing -
No promises -
No strings attached.

Spencer Redfield

AN OLD BEARDIE

I watch my Bonnie growing old,
in her life she's been like gold,
keeping me company winning shows,
never knowing how the years go,
from being a pup to full mature,
for Bonnie now has much a future,
for us to love her every day,
all we can give her along life's way,
we give her a little walk and play,
making sure she does not stray,
she sleep a lot eats her meal,
loves us both it's not unreal,
we kiss her on her nose each night,
and say Bonnie we love you - you're alright,
morning comes she looks at me,
telling me the night is through,
I say to her one day at a time,
we love you even if we say it in rhyme.

Teresa V Walker

TOGETHER

Man and maid walk hand in hand
Looking for their promised land
Seeing beauty everywhere
Building their castles in the air
The youth is the time when plans are made
With hope and sound foundations made
No thoughts of a cruel tomorrow
When one must beg, steal or borrow
Only thro' rose coloured spectacles see
A land of hope, peace and plenty.
Go see your world as you want it to be
For true to each other, that's the key
For love will make your world bright
You'll walk together into the light
Birds will sing, flowers bloom
No thought of sorrow or gloom
Oh lucky youth! How soon it goes
The years fly by as old age knows
So walk together as it should be
From youth unto eternity
Life will take you for good or ill
To your promised land where life stands still.

E Preston

THE WEDDING DRESS

I saw the wedding gown on display..
I went back for another glimpse - every single day!
I saw the gleam of stain - and the veil so frail and fair!
The sweet little rosebuds, and the silver horseshoes there!
I saw the veil, like a shimmering cloud!
And the dainty parasol, of which one would be proud!
I thought of another wedding - so military, warlike, austere in every way.
I heaved a sigh - for dreams gone by
'If only' I started to say -
But what of finery if love's not there?
I have all of this - I don't despair!

D Halliwell

YOU ARE A PART OF ME

Thou art more beautiful than the moon
Or a rainbow that is gone too soon
The colours that you bring and sine on me
Are more true and brighter than any I do see
How dull my life before you came
So still unmoving and all the same
I live my days for you alone
You are the heart that fills my home
And if you died my life would fold
I'd be so lost - so sad - so cold
And empty house without any life
Would cut me deep just like a knife
No warmth of breath upon my cheek
And where for comfort would I seek
So hold me close and feel me near
You are my love and one so dear
For without you where would I be
You're very much a part of me.

J Bedford

TO HAVE LOVED AND LOST

As I lie, on my big lonely bed,
I think of my love now gone.
My children all grown
And gone from the nest,
My life now - it's just second best!

Yet sorrow is dulled and I've time now to think,
Of the happiness over the years.
Why should I be sad?
Surely I should feel glad
That our days were so joyfully filled.

The past is over and life starts anew,
Fond memories crowding around.
Where now to go?
What new to do?
There's no-one to whom I am bound.

I don't have to be back for the washing,
Or cook a big family dinner.
No darning to do,
No beds to be made,
My own Mrs for once, and I'm slimmer.

Since I wrote that, I've travelled far.
Why save money for tomorrow?
The time for living
Is here and now.
There's no joy in living with sorrow.

So I say to the lonely, sincerely,
When grief has lost its sway,
Count your blessings,
Live life to the full.
What you've had, they can't take away.

Mabel Trumble

AXHOLME

How calm the isle
So flat and so still
Its peace now disturbed
By plough and the drill
Its rich waters drained of centuries past
Its rivers diverted for drainage to last.

The dark soil remembers
Ancient peat and fen
Its landscape now changed will not return again.
And once how enclosed by rivers and pools
Now replaced by roads with all of their rules.

How battles were fought
For rights to the land
As kings and their follies
Would not raise their hands
For monies were needed
And kings will have their way
Commoners' rights did not matter in that day.

Yet how calm the isle
With its history rich
And heavy black soil
In which secrets are hid.

John Todd

CHILDHOOD

The school bell rings,
Come in children it sings.

In they go full of glee,
A full day ahead but they're happy.

Register done it's time to play,
While away the hours is their way.

A childhood gone, I'm a woman now,
The pace of life gets quicker somehow.

My children make many demands on me,
Play a game mum I want my tea.

Bath time over a story to read,
Then there's a husband to feed.

Tucked up in bed all tired and worn,
Two little faces all smiley and warm.

My little girls smelling so sweet,
They're sugar and spice my own little treat.

So next time the kids are being bad,
Remember you've been blessed and be glad you have.

L A Riley

I WANT A JOB

The little girl cried out in pain
Daddy don't go away again,
But her father had no work you see,
He answered with sadness in his voice,
My little girl I have no choice
His wife's eyes glistened with tears
She understood all his fears
He tried to do his best in life,
And always took good advice
Maybe, he would say,
Things will turn out well some day.
It was such a shame
He died the next day
The following day to his wife's dismay
Came a letter from a job
Saying start today.

E J Green

SOLI GLORIA DEO

Just a little something to you
From all . . . in His glory
The new leaves are moving
So peacefully, covering the whole area
The whole life of the tree
Is so mild out there to me
Yet every single beautiful leaf
On that tree is always in motion
For a while each day this happens
May as well be every day
The trees never have to chase the wind
They belong to each other
The perfect everyday relationship
It's not the same wind I chase
Of course, how could it be?
Takes only this one bit of nature
And one quick glance of the eye
To be wonderfully reminded
Of what moves my leaves
And the nature of the wind
For us.

The wind I truly belong
My flesh continues to run from
All wind that's not of this world
In favour of . . .
Superficial cool breezes and the like
(Remote Controlled Robot Air Conditioning)
Thank our Maker for
Occasional hold-backs
To feel the inner breeze that
Turned my whole life upside down
For . . . for this
I've never been so grateful
For the wind with me.

'Soli Gloria Deo', (In God alone be Glory)
These are the last words
I'll ever speak
Everything's changed
I love!

Mike Stringer

ANOTHER WORLD

Star crossed astronaut feeling good,
Flag flying high, like it should.
Like neon beams his screen lit up bright,
Moon and stars clearly seen that night.
Another world reached, a safe touchdown,
Walking in a suit upon that alien ground.
Soon it's time to return to the ship,
Celebrating with a strong drink to sip.

David Powley

THE MAGNOLIA'S AWAKENING

A long grey-stone wall gives
Little comfort for seeing eyes
Across the way, until
A thin filter of light reveals
The charcoal image of candelabra
A blacksmith's dream for fair copy.

But what is this?

The sun getting stronger,
The sky getting bluer,
And in one single moment
The claret stained chalice
Of a myriad cream candles
Open up in one glorious display.

The seeing eyes across the way
Rejoice, and thank God or
Nature for lighting up the day.

I Scarlett

DUNROAMIN'

There's a good feeling about this house
We said
Love was here, is here -
Absorbed into the atmosphere
Who lived here do you think?
Happiness comes through the floor
And in the door
All around us - don't you think
We owe it to those here before
Our love and joy with theirs to store
While life is long?
Let's get the central heating on.

Jo Lee

SPRING

The lamb that takes the place of winter's roar,
Is full of hope, of happiness and life;
And all on earth take leave from fear and strife
Of winter's cold and bitter reign, and soar
Again to thoughts of sweeter things that be,
Of the beauty that is life's own pure key,
Of human love and truth that ever rise
When spring is born and winter dormant lies.

The snows, the fogs and keenest frosts are gone.
Green tender shoots burst through the fruitful earth,
As buds on stately trees take joyous birth
And birds sing out their hearts from early morn.
Primroses and daffodils blend colours bright
With blossoms white, and wallflowers gently fight
To disclaim their ugly name with sweetest scent.
And man awakes and is for once content.

A R Barnes

THE YOUNG ONES

People condemn the youth of today
For smoking and taking drugs.
But I wish they would stop and think
And not take the young ones for mugs
The vast majority are clever and kind
Work hard and help one another.
They won't go very far wrong
If loved by father or mother.
Growing up in this day and age
With all this computerisation
They take it all in their stride
Without a deal of frustration
It's our generation who must look at ourselves
And stop pulling young ones apart
But give them all the love that they need
And they will give from the heart.

J B Walshe

SAD

I'm very sad,
I think I'm slightly mad,
I have a sister called Stacie,
She drives me rather crazy,
She never does as she's told,
And she's slightly bold,
I guess she's rather selfish,
Which makes her very mad,
And me very sad.

Stephanie Lee (13)

DESTROYED

Reaching to the sky.
With a forest of golden leaves,
Which fall to the ground with the gentle
Autumn breeze,
With branches that reach for freedom,
Their lives about to be destroyed.

Elizabeth Harrison (9)

STRESS

The sun is moving in the west
The people they are thinking,
It is about what to do best
Before the sun is sinking.

People scurry here and there
In search of victuals to survive
The supermarket beckons all
Into the vast emporium.

With wire cage and nimble feet
It's round the aisles to find a treat
When all the goods have been collected,
Then to the checkout they are expected.

Life today is full of stress.
People seek; what do they seek?
A settled life with job secure
Is not too much to ask I'm sure.

Minds are troubled by our lives,
As day by day our work-load grows.
Let us turn inward with our minds
Until our imagination shows.

Then all our lives will better be
As calm our thoughts become,
And we will grow internally.
When each day, our work is done.

F W Leedham

THE ELEPHANT

Five blind men wanted to see,
What on earth was an *elephant*?

I'll go up said the first,
It's a tree,
He was holding a knee.

I'll go up said the second,
It's a rope,
He said in a wail,
He was holding the tail.

My turn said the third,
It's a wall, he cried,
He was pushing the side.

My turn now said the fourth,
It's just a fan here,
Pulling the elephant's ear.

I'm last again said the fifth,
I don't believe it,
It's like a snake he said with a thump,
Holding the trunk.

Claire Blagden

COAST

Electric blue lines speed through my memory
like the old asteroid space invader in the Regal.
Sticky, singed carpet tugs at my sole
as I enter the den of iniquity.
Eyes flash, grimace past the dancing puppet box,
limp corpses strung up, aching for the old 5p.
The seedy clown stares his paedophile smile
lusting for young laughter.
Cumbersome, aged machines lined up ready for metal,
round orange buttons, telling the tale
of a 1000 thumb prints.
Nudge, nudge, nudge . . . jackpot,
is that all? Oh I forgot you're old,
ageing like the concrete underneath.
Though you're younger than prom and sand,
oh, if each grain could talk of what it saw,
the dog's cocked leg, dropped ice-cream,
sweethearts heaving.
Do they remember the Victorian foot, the Viking stomp,
do they recall?
            Do they?

Andrea Fairweather

STEEL

Flow mighty torrents sparkle white
Through air and from the inside part
That has been plundered vilely chewed
From the green places of our youth

Was there no thought except to work
Brown earth to grey and stone to blade
In the long cathedrals of the New-God
Where there rocking tombs are laid?

There is a thunder newly wrought
Where fleshless creatures stretch their jaws
Push back the earth and deeply go
Into the raw unfinished soil.

The tumbrils waiting take their fill
From pit to pallid throats they flow
And turn the rock to molten forms
That only men of steel shall know.

In halls of darkness lit by fire
Stabbed by a thousand lights and shades
Where dust and smoke and ashes rise
Into a whole world aflame.

Yet stay a while and watch the fire
And the long steel rods flying
And the tall bars that shall stand erect
When the high priests are dying.

W E Hobson

LITTLE GREY DONKEY

Little grey donkey, how rough your coat,
How patient you stand while your nose I stroke,
But you are stubborn, or so they say,
You try every trick to get your own way.

But little grey donkey, please tell me do,
A donkey carried Mary to Bethlehem long ago,
Where Jesus was born, and in a manger laid,
While angels sang as shepherds prayed.

So why little donkey, your lowly estate?
All the hard tasks seem to be your fate,
Yet you were honoured above much bigger things,
For you have carried the King of Kings.

L M McIntyre

CHAMELEON

I perch here, waiting, like a fish
Out of water, not floundering
On this dry twig, in this green bush,
My body green, hard-pressed against
A rocking branch, my scaly back
Curved, low-arched above my belly
Flat-spread along the fleshy bark.
I squat. I perch. I balance. My
Colour is not of my essence:
Set me in blue, I am the blue;
In green, I have a green presence.
I am what my surroundings say
I am, perched here, eyes unblinking,
Waiting, a green reptile, unseen,
Fading, moving with the rocking
Of this branch. Only now and then,
A sticky tube, my tongue flicks out,
A flash of pink against the green,
Pricks an insect. Jaw rocks hard-shut
On tight-furled tongue. My wide eyes blink.
Then skin turns; satisfaction spreads.
Against the green, I set the pink.

Stan Downing

TO WINNIE

can you hear the tears drop
against the window pane
can you hear the heart beat
like a marching band?

listen.
if you really want to
you can even hear a pen drop
or the sound of screwed-up letters,
as yet unwritten,
hitting the waste-paper bin.

but can you measure
disappointment
disappearance
disillusionment
when the distance is unclear?
if you can answer that
try this for size:
how far is forever?
how heavy is a tear?
who can see the wind?
neither you nor i
but whichever way it blows
it can't blow me back again.

John Walters

POLITICS?

Labour, Tories, Lib Dem, Greens,
Does anyone know what politics means?
If one party's in, the others must be out,
But all they seem to do is moan, whinge and shout.

Conferences, summits, committees and quotas,
All designed to confuse the average voters.
Meeting OAP's and lots of baby kissing,
I'm sure they think our common-sense missing.

They lie and cheat, connive and scheme,
Just to achieve the party dream.
Promises, promises, from NHS to tax,
But what we can't see is crossed fingers
Behind their backs.

Vote for us to defend this land,
We won't let it fall into foreign hands.
Vote for us, you know we're good
And your family will never want for food.
Vote for us, don't stand on the border,
We're the party of law and order.
Vote for us we'll boost your wealth,
And give more money to the National Health.

The list of promises goes on and on,
Until after the election, then they're gone.
When they're elected and at their most senior,
They seem to contract acute amnesia.

We're been in office now for a few years,
And we understand the people's fears,
We know about the jobless, health and crime,
But please be patient,
We just haven't had time.

Garth Taggart

THE WORLD

The world around seems 'void of love', we hear and read such things
People stealing, no respect, all things decent they reject
The world around seems 'void of care' we hear and read such things
Selfishness and greed abound, why is it care is not around?
The world today is 'void of hope' we hear and read such things
Solemn news and sordid pictures, flood our television screens
Is there an answer to the need of this our world today?
The answer lies in God's great love, and we must learn to pray
And, having prayed we must believe, that God can all things do
Can conquer the impossible, and remain forever true
Yes! Love will conquer evil, and care and hope abound
Yes! Joy will surely follow, when we God's love have found.

F Merrett

NO CHILDHOOD DREAMS

Once I was given a flower, when the world was young.
When fairytales and wishing wells lifted hearts in song.
But now the flower is withered, the fairytales no more,
As this thing we call, 'progress', opens up another door.
Now everything is plastic, the computer age is nigh,
And so we go and pave the way for another flower to die.
No childhood dreams to guide the way with purity and light,
The flowers they cried their silent tears,
They fought but lost the fight.

Janine A Smith

CAMBRIDGESHIRE

The colleges of Cambridge are all well-known
And Cambridge is an interesting old town
The River Cam flows through, and shops to see
The river bank is a nice quiet place to be
In easy reach of the seaside but has no coast
Two cathedrals the county can boast
Peterborough and Ely have one each
From three airports are easy to reach
Ely has Cromwell's house as well
Peterborough has stories of Hereward to tell
Also has Queensgate Centre, the best around
And the town itself is an interesting town
The Key Theatre on the banks of River Nene
The old Guildhall and the market to be seen
The fens close by, were drained to make more land
To grown sugarbeet and potatoes, the best in England.

George E Woollard

JACK FROST

Jack Frost how cold and icy you are,
Hitting faces and hands with the icy tips
of your fingers,
Your face has icicles hung from it,
You're spiky and as cold as cold could be,
Jack Frost go away you're not welcome
here any day.

Hajar Javaheri (9)

MUMMY'S BOY

Our Damien is a terror
Although he's only six
The doctor says he's too advanced
Always up to tricks

He put super glue on his school friend's cups
It took hours to break the weld
The teachers got together
And now he is expelled.

He wanted to play firemen
So one warm July night
He crept into the garden
And set the summer house alight.

We told him we were very cross
As we rang the real firemen
And as an extra punishment
Now he goes to bed at ten.

We try not to get too cross with him
We never scream and shout
Just take him in a corner
And try to talk it out.

I've noticed lately when he grins
Perhaps there's nothing wrong
Two of his teeth on either side
Are starting to grow long.

Sometimes he is a treasure
As gentle as a pup
But one day like a treasure
He will have to be locked up.

Trevor Napper

MODERN LOVE AFFAIR

A time for loving and a time for lust
Backstreet bedsits in a neon glow
Take me now, for tonight is a must
But don't let my scars show.

The real wounds are inside our heads
A decade of healing
As they abuse our beds
Bodies become void of feelings.

Sting of lust in the morning light
Body lies broken on a blood stained quilt
'Your performance was epileptic last night'
There's no feelings of guilt.

Do we wonder at this state of decadence?
Is this a product of perverted mind?
I'm not embarrassed by your naked presence
Mother nature can be so unkind.

T J Sammons

LAND ARMY LILL

There is a lady quite close by, who in the
Land Army went, she drove the tractor, worked the
land her wages heaven spent.

She toiled all day and sometimes night for 30 bob
a week, her boss who was a mean old git took
15 bob for keep.

Her chosen trade was good hard work, she worked
from dust till dawn, she ploughed the fields and
milked the cows in her Land Army uniform.

While in this trade Lill met her match, and was
married still quite young. The years went by the
kids were born, 3 daughters and 1 son.

The outdoor life was all Lill knew, in sunshine
and in rain, she is still quite fit and still works
hard, the Land Army was her aim.

Sue Curtis

UNTITLED

Somewhere in the open sky
Like a mine blown up as time goes by,
The stars shine down and the universe lightens
The whole earth the moon does brighten.

Flaming spheres hovering by,
The end is near, the time is nigh.
I scream out loud for my life, may it be saved
This holocaust world I solemnly braved.

I reach out for mercy but no-one is there
The room is empty and the walls are all bare.
My voice echoes in the discomforting gloom
Knowing I sit alone in this dreary room.

In this candlelit hovel my life will end.
Me, alone without a friend.
Somehow, I can't turn back
And now my world is completely black.

Susan Lunn

SATURDAY NIGHT FEVER

A strange phenomenon has hit the UK,
Britain today is giving pounds away,
Millions, are parting with pounds every day.
The people pour their pounds,
Into, shops and supermarkets.
In exchange, they receive a piece of paper.
On which is printed, their six favourite numbers.
(Aunties' ages, birthdays, grannie's house-number)
Even on Saturdays, they can be seen, in,
Newspaper shops, getting their slips.

On Saturday nights, everyone gathers
Round a TV, the drawn numbers to see.
Excitement mounts to fever pitch,
As the last number comes out.
There is an expectant hush, as slips are checked.

Groans come from the losers,
But a shout of joy from a winner,
As he punches the air with his fist.

It makes a few million for you and me,
And a bit for charity.

The government and organisers, get a share,
I suppose that's only fair!
Because you see, it's the National Lottery.

T Leech

WILD CHERRY

Translucent - ethereal -
A breath-taking sight,
The little tree stands there
A cascade of white
Blossom on blossom
Transformed in the night.

Its beauty so fragile -
When the winds blow
The petals come whirling
Like small flakes of snow
And cover so gently
The green grass below.

This transient beauty
Will soon disappear,
But the miracle happens
Year after year
And transforms a tree
That is humble and plain
To a vision of beauty
Again and again.

Margaret Parry

WAITING FOR YOU (SEEMS LIKE THIS NEVER ENDS)

Waiting for you
Seems like this never ends
Will you ever grow up and leave home
and make me proud
then I'll just sink into the background
Wishing I wasn't famous
I'll wonder why I was in a rush
But this waiting around is bringing me down
If you were a 'real' child the pregnancy would be long over
But you're just a book
Worth a second look
I know you'll eventually go
and the life I crave will flow
But until then I'll just want to know
and my gratitude to those who get us there
I will always show
Waiting for you
I've just got to think positive
I know that you're strong enough to work
and that one day you'll be published
My wait will then end.

A J Hayward

WHEN I AM GONE

When I am gone they'll see my bed
Its sagging mattress - enough said.
When I am gone they'll see my sink
'Ye gods' they'll say 'it makes you blink.'

When I am gone they'll see my chairs
Its busted springs, not worth repairs
When I am gone they'll see my mats,
My shabby clothes, my dated hats.

When I am gone they'll search for money
Trouble is - I haven't any.

D Maltby

THE AWAKENING

Wakes now the sun's warm kiss the dormant earth;
Stirs the reluctant soul to life again;
Now swells the gentle air to symphony,
Notes sweet to pain:
So fill the vessel, even to the brim:
Come pain or joy, lifts up the soul her lips
To drink again.

Now must she drink, and thirst, to drink again
And find all beauty in a moment's span;
All joy, all wonder, mirrored in the cup,
Be it blessing or bane;
Whether it hold of grief or ecstasy:
Come pain or joy, she stand with outstretched hands
And trembles on the brink of mystery.

Daphne Foreman

THE PLACE

The place is a narrow footpath
Leading upwards. It is late summer
On one side a field slopes down
To a lake edged with rushes,
On the other, a copse of hazel bushes,
Tall grass brushes against us as we pass,
A burr of knapweed catches on my skirt
A bee out late is looking for a flower
And everywhere the smell of hay.
This is how I remember it,
For it is many years since I went that way
Walking in the evening with my mother.
Yet this memory more than any other
Stays fresh and clear,
I shut my eyes and I am young again
And in that place
With the smells of summer
And the breeze on my face.

Freda L MacColl

MY FUNDAY OUT

Today is Sunday.
It's my funday.
I want to go to the zoo.
The one in Smyton, it's very new.

They have a very big brown bear
It gives some people a scare
They have a collection of wild cats
But you don't want to give them strokes or pats.

There are ten tall giraffes
But please don't knit them scarves.
There are sixty strong does and deer
They are very shy, they won't come near.

Oh look at that cute seal.
'Quick Mum! My shoulders are starting to peel.'
Elephants suck things out of your hand
And sometimes scare your old nan.

Next week we're going to the pier.
But first today, before I go, I want a souvenir.

Sharron Munday (9)

IN EVERY HUMAN BEING THERE IS A POET STRUGGLING TO EMERGE

The human animal has an active mind
And it's healthy to allow it to roam
But of all the pursuits it becomes involved in,
The most rewarding is writing a poem.

The voice is for speaking or singing a song
Be it 'pop' or 'Oh Tannenbaum'
But the brain can direct anyone's hand
To be dextrous in writing a poem.

So whether at home, in the city or town,
Abroad or just crossing the 'foam'
Always find a few moments to be by yourself
To relax and compose a poem.

You may visit the capital of our fair land
And be awe-struck by St Paul's great dome.
If the 'Whispering Gallery' enthuses you
Write your thoughts in the form of a poem.

An habitual reader you may well be,
So the next time you complete a tome
Use it as the base for intelligent thought
And convert it into a poem.

The diminutive spirits of subterranean race;
Salamander, sylph, nymph and gnome,
Guard the most precious treasures of our earth
So honour their work in a poem.

In spite of your travels to work or abroad
You'll spend most of your leisure at home.
There's no finer training of a person's mind
Than to sit down and write a poem.

John W Skepper

ODE TO A BUTTERFLY

Beautiful creature with iridescent wings
Where do you stand in the order of things?
Like the morning glory that blooms for a day,
You show us your beauty then take it away.

Your humble beginning, in just one day,
Evolves to a beauty no art could portray.
You appear in the morning, spread your wings to the light,
Then when shadows appear close them up again tight.

As you flutter round gardens and vie with each flower
You grow more languid with each passing hour.
There are those who would covet your beauty and grace
And pin you for ever behind glass in a case.

P J Anderson

TRAPPED BY WORDS

Words are dangerous things,
No one has complete command,
'I didn't mean that'
Words can destroy while the mind free wheels,
Is the meaning conveyed in words or do words restrict the meaning?
The colander that has no restraint on infinity confines the definition of words,
Words are a poor medium by which to express thought,
Their inaccuracy is off the scale,
Perception/emphasis are whims of an individual - sentries employed by words to confine the purest of thought,
While words are a necessity - rule words by thought - keep some thought untouched by words lest they be adulterated,
Think in visions - think in music but do not get trapped by words,
If you claim to understand my words you are a cold liar,
If you have the faintest following of the meaning behind my words my thoughts have conquered,
Tell me for you are truly my friend and can help me break free from the prison of my words.

Reuben Semple

BLOOD, SWEAT AND TEARS
(Initiation of a girl vampire)

Blood drips from her cherry red lips,
Sharp white teeth smothered with saliva,
Eyes once blue now black with evil,
His blood swells her greedy veins.

Sweat trickles down her heaving breasts,
Claw-like nails digging into skin,
Heart once pure now black with evil,
His flesh feeds her bloody desire.

Tears stream across her pale white cheeks,
Blood drenched tonguc caressing over wounds,
Mind once sound now black with evil,
His pain satisfies her nasty need.

S L Jackson

FRIENDS BESIDE US

When friends walk beside us,
On the trails that we keep.
Our burdens will be less heavy,
And hills not so steep.
Weary miles pass swiftly,
Taken in joyous stride,
And all the world seems brighter,
When friends walk by our side.

Sylvano Cassingena

WHERE WOULD I BE?

I used to feel bitter
about this town,
But in the space of
a week
My views have changed
It is a place to live,
There is a society,
Tourists visit, I
understand why,
This town has history,
memories of past years.
This town also has present time.
It is still alive with the
activity of people
Living here now.
Where would I be
without this town?

Fiona Stimpson (17)

REINCARNATION

Once we were in one womb,
No matter when.
And if we meet again
Across what wild water,
Or clash of culture,
Not loving or liking,
But knowing,
In eye's meeting.
Beyond memory,
Or similarity,
But recognising,
Speaking one language
Made of moods,
And unseen nods.
No need of kisses,
For they come later,
No need of words,
They are not better
Than bubbles
In the amniotic water.

Vera Boyle

INFORMATION

We hope you have enjoyed reading this book - and that you will continue to enjoy it in the coming years.

If you like reading and writing poetry drop us a line, or give us a call, and we'll send you a free information pack.

Write to

Anchor Books Information
1-2 Wainman Road
Woodston
Peterborough
PE2 7BU